STUDENT ENGAGEMENT MANTRAS

DR DHEERAJ MEHROTRA
MADHUKAR NARRAIN

Contents

Preface

Friends welcome to the world of learning. Engagement happens when students care about the material, feel welcome in the classroom, understand expectations, and have fun. When we think of student engagement in learning activities, it is often convenient to understand engagement with an activity as being represented by good behaviour (i.e., behavioural engagement), positive feelings (i.e. emotional engagement), and, above all, student thinking (i.e., cognitive attention) (Fredricks, 2014).

*The book featuring **Student Engagement Mantras** shares some strategies to harness their learning in reality!*

Happy Learning.

Dr Dheeraj Mehrotra

Madhukar Narrain

ONE

Student Engagement Mantras

Dear Students,

Learning is a priority, and it comes with engagement. What is more important is an improvement with the march of time. Here comes the importance of KAIZEN!

Kaizen is a Japanese term meaning "change for the better" or "continuous improvement." It is a Japanese business philosophy regarding the processes that continuously improve operations and involve all employees. Kaizen sees improvement in productivity as a gradual and systematic process. The concept of kaizen encompasses a wide range of ideas. It makes the work environment more efficient and effective by creating a team atmosphere, improving everyday procedures, ensuring employee engagement, and making a job more fulfilling, less tiring, and safer.

♡♡♡

Good manners or MANTRAs are related to priority towards excellence. Get them now to explore your personality for the best for life!!

Cheers!

MANTRA #1

Prepare yourself to learn: You need to be prepared for learning. Without preparations, you cannot know. If you fail to PLAN, you PLAN to fail.

MANTRA #2

Gather the resources for learning: Learning involves reading, writing, listening, watching, and practising. You need to have books, notebooks, videos, podcasts and webcasting. Cash on WWW- Whatever, Whenever, Wherever learning policy.

MANTRA #3

Shake off your anxiety and stress. If your mind is anxious and stressful, you cannot learn. You can know well only when your mind is at peace. Have joy while Learning.

MANTRA #4

Get some exercise: Exercise helps you maintain your physical and mental health. If you are not healthy, you learn slowly.

MANTRA #5

Eat a balanced diet for better learning: You cannot learn when your stomach is empty, and you will also not be able to know if you have overeaten. Eat-in short intervals but not all at once!

MANTRA #6

Boost your mental capacity: To learn, your brain should function properly. Your brain will work better if you use it more. You have to use your brain to think, contemplate and analyse.

MANTRA #7

Take a brain supplement: You can boost your brain by taking brain supplements or foods that enhance memory. Teachers often suggest DARK CHOCOLATES for better memory!

MANTRA #8

Sleep well for better learning: There has been researching on how good sleep helps better understand and think analytically. Rest for 8 hours, work for 8 hours but not the same 8 hours!

MANTRA #9

Develop deep concentration: You need to concentrate on lessons to learn them. Without attention, you cannot know. Explore learning by understanding the content as a story. Make use of ICT – the videos to explore the learning topic-wise.

MANTRA #10

Take a break to learn better: Taking a break from your everyday life boosts your creativity and mental capacity. Long study hours will not help you in learning.

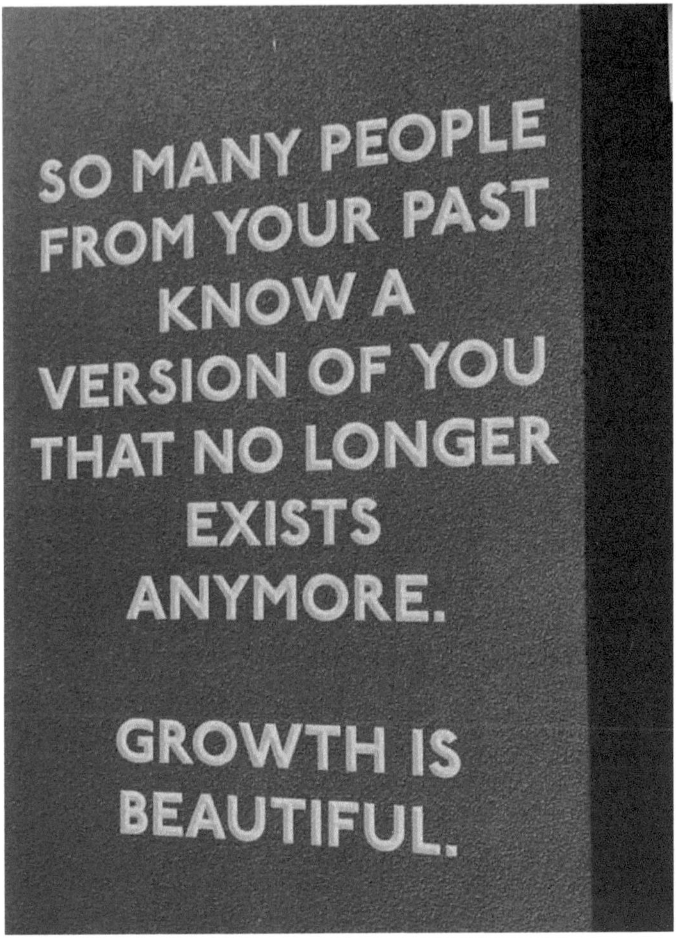

SO MANY PEOPLE
FROM YOUR PAST
KNOW A
VERSION OF YOU
THAT NO LONGER
EXISTS
ANYMORE.

GROWTH IS
BEAUTIFUL.

MANTRA #11

Explore Outdoor activities: Activities such as strolling in a garden, going for a walk or being with your pet for a while will relax you. When you are relaxed, you will learn better.

MANTRA #12

Change your focus: Studying the same subject again and again will only create monotony. To break that monotony, you need to change your subject quite often; for instance, you can switch between science and arts.

MANTRA #13

Reading: Reading is the most common method of learning. If you want to learn something, you have to read about it. Browse the NET, read newspapers or post on social networking. News on apps is not exceptional even.

MANTRA #14

Rereading: One-time reading may not help you understand everything; you have to reread for better understanding. The second reading will give you a better MANTRA, even more than the third. This applies to your notes and chapters.

MANTRA #15

Speed reading: Reading will help you learn; however, you can understand better by speed reading. Research has proved that people know better if they do speed reading.

MANTRA #16

Analytical thinking: To learn something, you need to have analytical thinking. Analytical thinking means you analyse the MANTRA carefully.

MANTRA #17

Learning by listening: A baby learns a word by listening. Listening is the primary method of learning. Listen before you speak.

MANTRA #18

Learning from the environment: The environment is a great teacher. You can learn so many things from the surrounding.

MANTRA #19

Developing interest: You won't learn anything until you are interested in it. For instance, if you are not interested in math, you will never learn math.

5 THINGS
Great Leaders Do Daily

H Be **HANDS-ON** with their team.

E Work on their **EMOTIONAL INTELLIGENCE.**

A Take **ACCOUNTABILITY** and ownership.

R Build positive **RELATIONSHIPS** and **RELATABILITY.**

T Create **TRANSFORMATION** in their team.

RISELEADERSHIPCOURSE.COM

MANTRA #20

Exploration: If you want to learn, you have to explore. Exploring means examining something and analysing it thoroughly.

MANTRA #21

Research: Researching is a great way to learn. When you research something, you will know about it. Practice CURATING knowledge.

MANTRA #22

Learning from elders: The elders have lived more years. Therefore, they know things better. You can learn so many things from your elders. RESPECT them, honour them and learn from them.

MANTRA #23

She is learning from young ones: People more youthful than you can also teach you so many things because every person is unique and intelligent in their ways.

MANTRA #24

Classroom learning: Classroom learning refers to attending school, college and training centres for formal education. Formal education is the most popular learning method. You always need a facilitator to learn and explore knowledge. Try taking the maximum through queries.

MANTRA #25

Distance learning: You can get a formal education by attending schools and college. However, if you cannot participate in schools or colleges, you can still learn through distance education. Distance education refers to learning from home. Even online learning: The best option to explore via UDEMY, COURSERA, LYNDA, EDX and others.

MANTRA #26

Online schools: Recently, online training and education are becoming very popular. You can enrol in online schools, universities, and training institutes to get a degree or diploma online.

MANTRA #27

Learning from the real world: The actual world is the best classroom to learn various things. You have to be a keen observer to learn from the real world.

MANTRA #28

Study: To learn, you have to study. Studying does not only mean virtual/real classroom looking; studying also refers to learning by self-study. Always keep and refer to some books apart from your TEXT or prescribed books.

MANTRA #29

Innovative learning: To learn, you need to study. However, you should also have the right approach to studying. It would help if you acquired clever studying techniques. Learn to browse smart. Blog your queries and showcase your social presence via putting questions.

MANTRA #30

Online discussion boards: Online forums can provide a good platform for building knowledge and skills. Get going with your ONLINE REPUTATION MANAGEMENT by posting and hosting the ability of your interest.

MANTRA #31

Blogs and websites: Blogs and websites provide an excellent resource for learning various things, from simple things such as writing an essay to complicated things such as web programming.

MANTRA #32

Online search: Search engines like Google can help you research any topics and provide you with resources on anything you want to learn. Use some more search engines and be an innovator and a contributor to learning through contribution to Wikipedia!

MANTRA #33

Learning from videos: Seeing is believing. Therefore, you will understand better from instructional and educative videos than from a classroom lecture. Upload your YouTube videos and even comment on those you watch and share!

MANTRA #34

Learning from audio media: Technology has created audiobooks; now, you don't have to read books to learn; you can listen to books. Audiobooks and podcasts are great tools for learning.

MANTRA #35

You are learning from Peers. Take the best from your friends, colleagues, relatives and teachers. Share and explore the learning to the best of use and meaning.

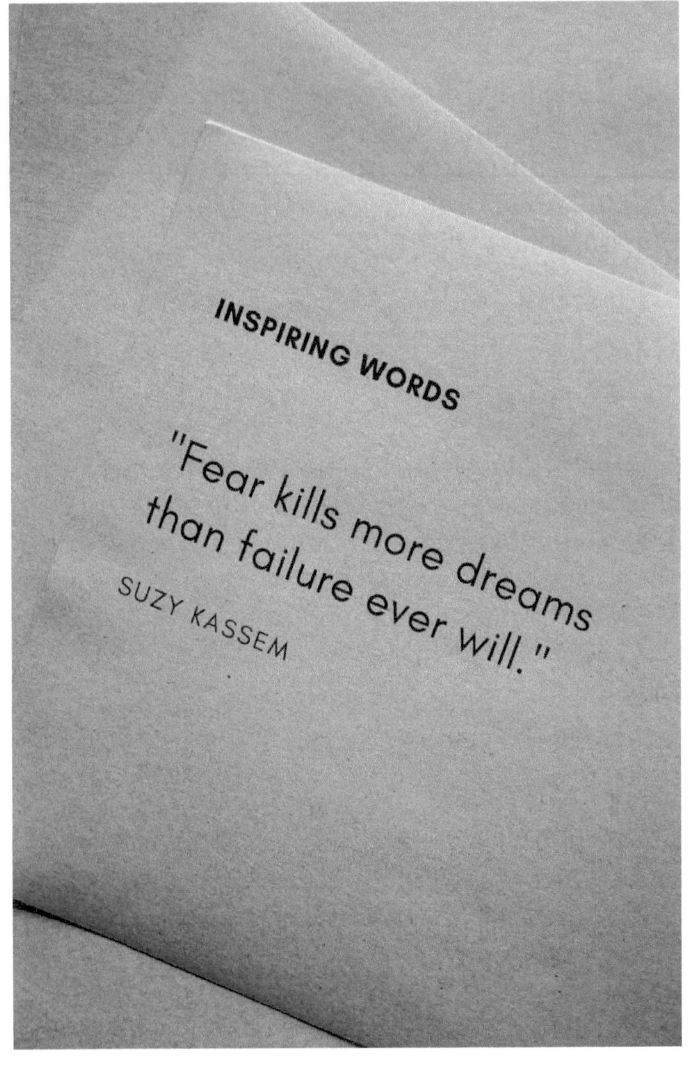
INSPIRING WORDS
"Fear kills more dreams than failure ever will."
SUZY KASSEM

MANTRA #36

Social Media: You might be using social media for fun, but have you realised the potential of social media in learning? Get a page of your chosen topic and explore learning through sharing and re-posting.

MANTRA #37

Group collaboration: Form small learners and give them something to contemplate. Shuffle the group members and let them discuss the same MANTRA. Use brainstorming to generate MANTRAs and share knowledge.

MANTRA #38

Question and Answer sites: Ask, Yahoo answers, and Quora are some of the questions and answer sites that can answer your questions.

MANTRA #39

Using iTunes for learning: iTunesU is an Apple platform for distributing podcasts, videos, apps, and other digital media in various categories. These media are great learning tools.

MANTRA #40

Smartphone Apps: You can find many learning apps on Google Play and the Apple store. You can find these learning apps for free or by paying little money.

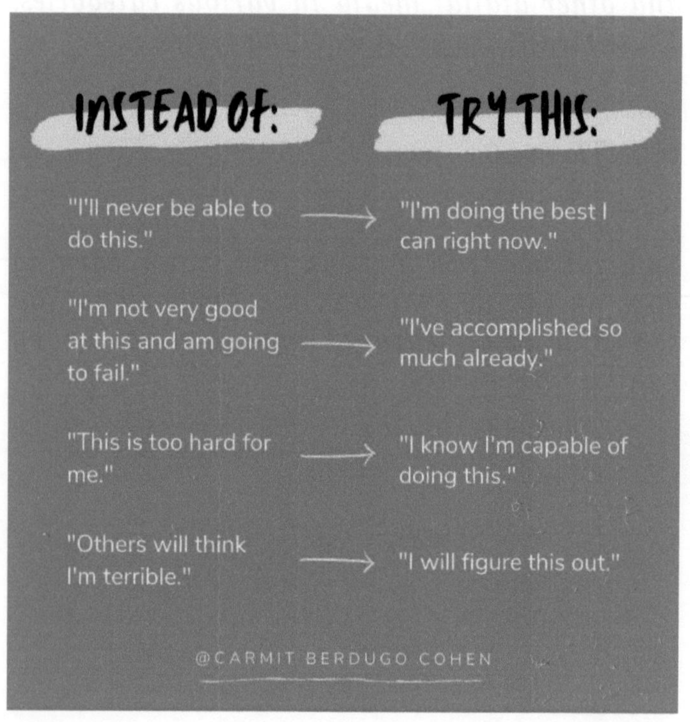

Source: Internet

MANTRA #41

Active learning: Active learning means the learners are involved with interactive problem solving by sharing MANTRAs and skills.

MANTRA #42

Self-directed learning: By evaluating your performance, you can learn many things. When you analyse your performance, you will know your strength and weakness.

MANTRA #43

Innovative learning: Innovation refers to creating something new through study and experimentation. If you are creative, you will always learn something new.

MANTRA #44

Learning through role-playing: Roleplaying will teach you through self-direction, experimentation, and practice.

MANTRA #45

Brainstorming is one of the best ways to develop a mantra or elaborate the MANTRA. Brainstorming can be done singly or in a group.

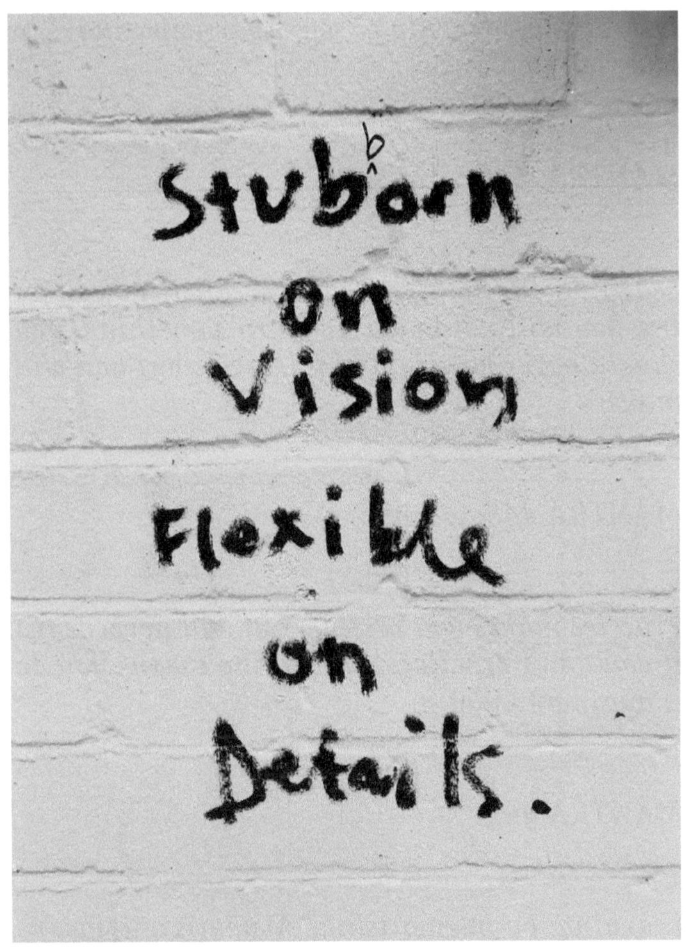

MANTRA #46

Interactive learning: Learners can engage with interactive learning by participating in question and answer sessions.

MANTRA #47

Learning through trial and error: If you don't try, you will not know. To learn something, you should never be afraid of mistakes that you will make.

MANTRA #48

Practice makes you perfect: You will never learn if you don't practice. Preparation means you do it again and again.

MANTRA #49

Learning by memorising: Memorizing means repeating something in your mind repeatedly and recording it so you can recall it when needed.

MANTRA #50

Learning from a storyboard: Storyboard is an excellent method of learning lessons that require memorisation and visual interpretations. Storyboard uses infographics, images, and stories.

A
DREAM
written down with a date becomes a
GOAL
A goal broken down into steps becomes a
PLAN
A plan backed by
ACTION
makes your dreams
REALITY

MANTRA #51

Learning from stories: Learning will be fun and effective if the lessons are introduced as stories. The storytelling technique can be used for children as well as adults.

MANTRA #52

Learning through stimulation: Stimulation refers to an act of arousing people to act. It will be easier to impart knowledge by stimulating the learners' minds.

MANTRA #53

Welcome new MANTRAs: To learn, your mind must be open to new MANTRAs. With a closed mind, you will never learn new things.

MANTRA #54

Learning from your hobbies: Your hobbies can also help you learn. Think about what your interests are, and then explore your interests.

MANTRA #55

Learning by solving puzzles and word games: You are always learning something new, a new word or information.

MANTRA #56

Board games: Board games are fun and help in analytical thinking. You can play chess not just for fun but also develop strategies.

MANTRA #57

Learning by playing games: Outdoor and indoor games will help the learners to think creatively, solve problems, and face challenges.

MANTRA #58

School/college clubs: School and college clubs can provide a learner with a platform to form a team with peers and exchange MANTRAs and knowledge.

MANTRA #59

Book clubs: By joining a book club, a learner will be introduced to the vast knowledge of the books. Book clubs also provide a platform for mutual exchange of MANTRAs and expressions.

MANTRA #60

Do what you want to do: You will learn only when you love it; if you don't love science, you will never learn anything about science. To learn, you have to love it. When you love the subject, you become more creative.

MANTRA #61

Creative Learning methods: To learn, the Learner should introduce innovative LEARNING methods like audio/video, multimedia, etc. Uploading videos on YOUTUBE and watching them for learning outcomes and feedback.

MANTRA #62

Learning from newspapers and magazines: Newspapers and magazines are the sources of news, information, and knowledge.

MANTRA #63

Learning from the radio: Because of its reach and flexibility, the radio is an excellent source of learning. You know a great deal by listening to informative and educative radio programs.

MANTRA #64

Learning from TV: TV is a popular entertainment medium for people of all ages. However, you should also realise the learning potential of TV.

MANTRA #65

Powerpoint presentations and slideshows: It is easier to learn when the lessons are introduced through PowerPoint presentations and slideshows.

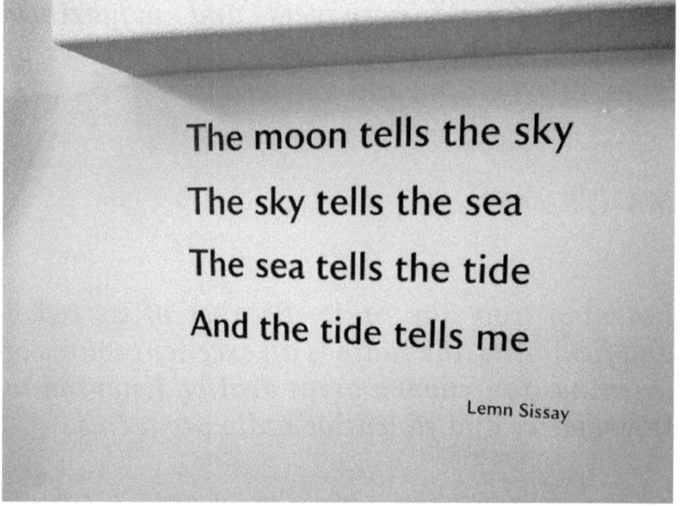

MANTRA #66

Comic strip: People learn better if drawings are used to explain the lesson. Comic strips provide a better understanding of lessons.

MANTRA #67

Learning through the survey: Survey not only gathers information from the participants but also helps in concluding.

MANTRA #68

Watching documentaries: Documentaries are audio-visual presentations of facts and events. The documentary helps in better understanding.

MANTRA #69

Museums: By visiting museums, a learner will learn more about history, art, and culture than by reading books.

MANTRA #70

Going to the exhibitions: Exhibitions are open classrooms to learn so many things. You will learn about art by visiting an art exhibition; by visiting a photography exhibition, you will learn about photography.

MANTRA #71

Learning by writing: You know better if you write it down. Writing is a great way to understand or memorise something.

MANTRA #72

Meditation: Research has proved that meditation develops mind power and concentration. Meditation is a way to tap into your inner resources and strengthen your ability to concentrate.

MANTRA #73

Change your learning methods: If one learning method is not working for you, change it. For example, if you cannot grasp books, watch educational videos.

MANTRA #74

Immerse yourself in learning: When you are learning, immerse yourself fully. Watching a TV and reading a lesson cannot go hand in hand.

MANTRA #75

Lose yourself: If you are uptight, you will never better understand the subject matter. Don't take learning as a burden.

MANTRA #76

Recall understanding better: To grasp the lesson, you must be able to recall it. You can be unable to identify means you did not understand properly.

MANTRA #77

Acronyms and mnemonic devices help better understand: Acronyms and mnemonic devices are tricks to memorise information and facts. By using these devices, you will be able to recall what you have learned.

MANTRA #78

A picture worth a thousand words: An image has so many things to tell; if you can associate a picture with something, it will be easier to learn.

MANTRA #79

Learning through brain map: A brain map is a way to get an overview of something. Brain mapping will help you to see the connections between different MANTRAs and utilise brainstorming techniques.

MANTRA #80

Learning from symbolism and semiotics: If you understand symbolism and semiotics, it will not help in the learning process but also assist you in retaining information efficiently.

MANTRA #81

Learn by mapping your task flow: Generally speaking, it requires acquiring knowledge in a specific sequence. If you can organise your thoughts on what needs to be done, you can prepare to complete the tasks and know "how to learn."

MANTRA #82

Get inspiration: Inspiration invokes your creativity. Stimulation invokes your efficiency. You need the motivation to become better at learning something.

MANTRA #83

Develop optimism: Optimism matters in life, even more in learning. Optimism will help you get involved in education. You are a better learner if you are an optimist.

MANTRA #84

State of happiness helps in learning: If you are a happy person, you excel in education. A sad person or a pessimist individual will always fail in understanding.

MANTRA #85

Stimulate MANTRAs: To make yourself more receptive to learning, you must stimulate MANTRAs. You can boost MANTRAs by playing rhyming games, word association, or stream-of-consciousness.

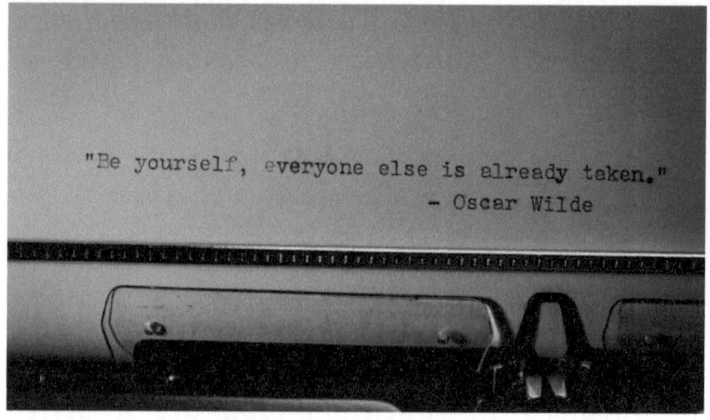

MANTRA #86

Learn super learning methods: Scientists and educationists have developed excellent learning methods. Research these great learning methods and use the one most appropriate for you.

MANTRA #87

Learning through binaural beats: Binaural beats is a super learning method. In this learning method, two different frequencies are played simultaneously to produce feelings, including alertness and concentration.

MANTRA #88

Carry a notepad: Thoughts and MANTRAs are like sea waves; they come and go. You need a tablet to record your thoughts; even your phone's pad will work. By registering, you can easily recall.

MANTRA #89

Keep a journal: Journals are different from notepads. On note pads, your thoughts and MANTRAs are essential; in your journal, you can explore these thoughts and MANTRAs. You can add visual details, charts, brain maps, etc., to your journal. A serial will help you keep track of your learning process.

MANTRA #90

Write books on a topic you like the most. This shall develop your passion for the subject and the content. Be a lifelong learner.

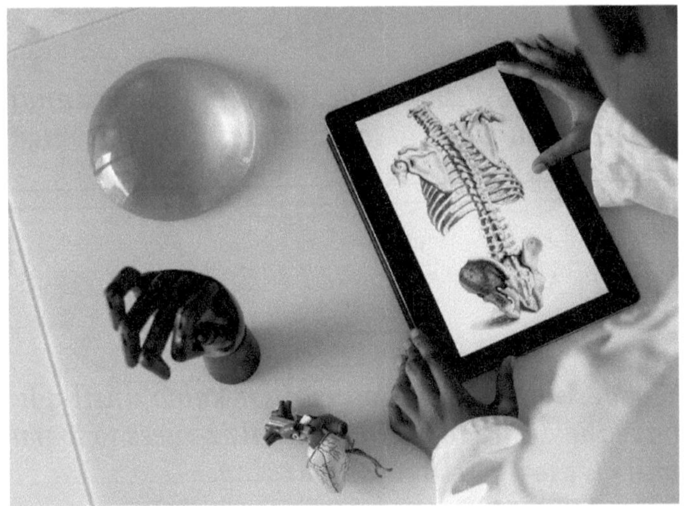

MANTRA #91

Any time is the right time: There is no wrong time for learning. If you want to learn, you can start learning at any time. Socrates was trying to learn how to play a musical instrument even though he was sentenced to death.

MANTRA #92

Dedication: Without dedication, you cannot learn. If you want to learn something, you must be a dedicated learner.

MANTRA #93

The desire to learn: You cannot know until you have the desire to learn. The willingness to learn will create a passion for learning.

MANTRA #94

Motivation: You need the inspiration to learn; without cause, you cannot know or become a slow learner. Reasons also keep the distractions away.

MANTRA #95

Find the purpose of learning: If you have a sense, you can learn better. If you discover "why you want to learn," you become a better learner.

You can
WIN
if you
WANT

MANTRA #96

Set a goal: Having a plan helps you learn better. You should have answers to the question like "what do you want to achieve through learning?"

MANTRA #97

Every skill can be learned: There is nothing impossible; you can know any skill. All you need is motivation and dedication.

MANTRA #98

Exercise self-control: All want enjoyment in life. However, life is not all about fun. There are things you should learn to make life better. Therefore every learner needs to exercise self-control.

MANTRA #99

Learn how to learn: One of the best ways is to learn how to learn. Find out various learning methods and apply the plan that best suits you.

MANTRA #100

Learn what you know and what you don't: No one is dumb. You know many things that others don't know. To learn something, you should know what you already know. You can never forget what you don't know.

ᑭᑭᑭ

MANTRA #101

Become a better learner by multitasking: Multitasking does not mean you watch the TV while reading the book. Multitasking means doing similar things at the same time. For instance, you can start learning two different subjects simultaneously.

MANTRA #102

Apply a holistic approach: You can learn better through a holistic approach. Holistic thinking is the most advanced learning technique to learn new things.

MANTRA #103

Learn through repetition: To grasp a new theory or a new subject, you need to study again and again. Repetition will help to absorb the concept.

MANTRA #104

Apply the Quantum Learning model: The Quantum Learning model uses foundation, atmosphere, environment, design, and delivery to impart knowledge and skills.

MANTRA #105

Get necessary tools: You can learn better if you have the right tool. Books are a primary source of learning. However, you should also use other tools like podcasts, videos, multimedia etc.

MANTRA #106

Learn through critical thinking: You need critical thinking in life, even more in your learning process. Critical thinking will develop your analytical skills and help your ability to learn.

MANTRA #107

Learn complex problem solving: Your ability to solve complex problems will help you manage your life and learn better.

MANTRA #108

Engage: Learning is not just reading books or listening to lectures. Learning is about participating in the discussion and asking and answering questions.

MANTRA #109

Using information pyramids to learn: The learning process goes through various steps. Learning always adds layers. You learn alphabets; you learn words; you learn sentences. Add advanced concepts to your learning pyramids.

MANTRA #110

Learning from video games: Video game has a bad reputation because the market is glutted with violent, non-educative games. However, you can find many educational games that help in effective learning.

ÞÞÞ

MANTRA #111

Go beyond the curriculum: A school/college goer should indeed excel in the school curriculum. However, there are many things to learn from the real world.

MANTRA #112

Learn from the real-life experience: Classroom learning is meaningful. However, the knowledge you gather from a classroom is never enough. You should learn from real-life experience.

MANTRA #113

Applied learning: You learn from a traditional or online classroom; however, if you cannot use your knowledge, you are just ignorant. Know how to apply what you have learned.

MANTRA #114

Teach yourself: You should never depend on instructors and teachers to learn. By teaching yourself, you will be equipped with the basic knowledge that helps the learning process.

MANTRA #115

Start blogging: Now, this might surprise you. However, creating a blog and publishing what you have learned will help you understand the concepts better and help others learn from what you have learned.

MANTRA #116

Quiz yourself: You have learned something, but realise how much you have absorbed the concept. By quizzing yourself, you will find out what you have learned and help to recall what you have learned.

MANTRA #117

Learn the basic things: You cannot learn a word without knowing the alphabet. Therefore, start with the basic concept and gradually reinforce your knowledge.

MANTRA #118

Persistence: Thomas Edison once said, "Genius is 1% inspiration and 99% perspiration". Never give up on learning. Don't be intimidated.

MANTRA #119

Challenge yourself: Generally speaking, you are more intelligent than you realise. Attempt to do something you have never done; you will discover your true potential.

MANTRA #120

Don't be afraid of castigation: The world is full of cynics. There are people around us who always try to downgrade us. Don't be scared of people who criticise you.

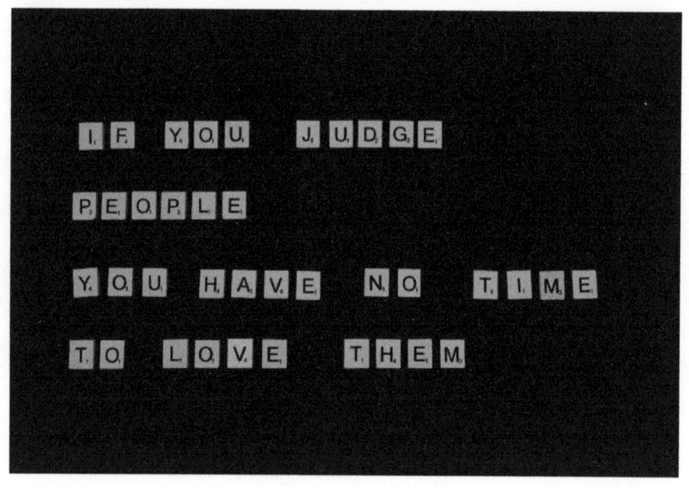

ᓚᓚᓚ

MANTRA #121

Don't be afraid of failures: It is impossible to succeed in every walk of life. Failures are a part of our life. There is nothing like a failure but FEEDBACK!

MANTRA #122

Party before an exam: Don't take "party" in a literal sense. Partying refers to relaxation. Cramming on the subject before the exam is not going to help you excel in the exams. Review what you have learned throughout the semester and sit relaxed.

MANTRA #123

Learning from animation: Research has proved that people know better if the lessons are introduced through animation videos. For better learning, energy should be combined with lectures and textbooks.

MANTRA #124

Learning through multimedia: Using projectors and slide shows, trainers and educators can make learning fun. Conversely, the learners are eager to know if the lessons are introduced through multimedia/ digital learning.

MANTRA #125

Learning from workshops: The workshop is a brief intensive course for a small group of learners emphasising problem-solving.

MANTRA #126

Do the hard work: You will learn only when you work hard—hardworking means studying the subject matter and practising the lesson learned.

MANTRA #127

Work smart: For effective learning, you need to work smart. Working bright implies using the right tools to study.

MANTRA #128

Result-oriented learning: Learning should always be substantial. If you are never rearing a cow, there is no point in learning how to raise a cow.

MANTRA #129

Learning skills: You will understand better only when you have learning skills. You must develop skills like concentration, reading and listening, remembering, time management, etc.

MANTRA #130

Gather and assess information: If you are learning something, gather as much information as possible, analyse the data, and interpret it insightfully.

ᑭᑭᑭ

MANTRA #131

Relate what you have learned: You learn to make your life better. Your knowledge is for your life. Relate what you have learned to your real life.

MANTRA #132

Understand the requirement of the institution: To learn, you enrol in an institution. Every institution has its requirement condition, such as attendance, assignments, participation in the discussion etc.

MANTRA #133

Think about the subject: Learning is never limited to one topic; you have to learn about various issues: Think about the subject you are studying. In a history class, think about past events; in a biology class, think about animals and plants.

MANTRA #134

Look for interconnections: Subjects are interconnected. History is connected with culture and politics. Science is associated with math. For effective learning, you need to see the subjects as interconnected.

MANTRA #135

Try to understand, rather than memorising: Of course, some things need to be remembered; however, for effective learning, you need to understand. When you know, you can learn it.

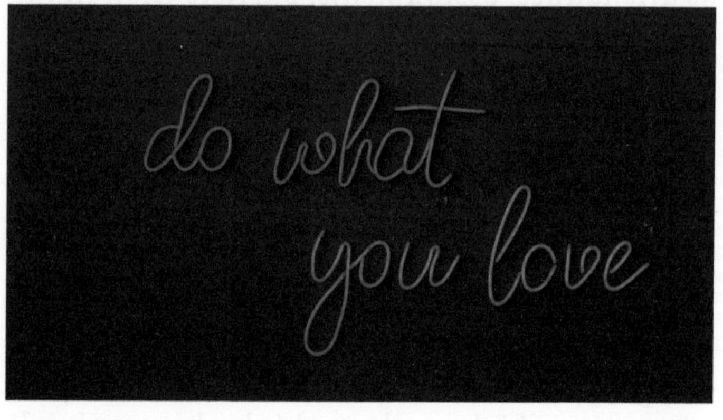

MANTRA #136

Have faith in your instructor: If you doubt your instructor, you will never learn anything from him. Your instructor is your coach to guide you through the depth of knowledge.

MANTRA #137

Figure out your weakness: Find out what you find most challenging. Study the subject more, practice the lesson and develop your knowledge.

MANTRA #138

Seek to find the key concept: When learning a subject, try to find the key concepts. Once you know what the issue is all about, you will develop the ability to improve your understanding.

MANTRA #139

Evaluate your listening skills: You actively listen to the lecture; do you understand everything he has said? When the course stops, you must be able to summarise the key points. You can do this only when you are an active listener.

MANTRA #140

Evaluate your reading skills: If you are reading a textbook, do you understand what you have read? Reading is connected with understanding. You need to know what you are reading.

ᑭᑭᑭ

MANTRA #141

Create a study schedule: For effective learning, you need to create a study schedule. Creating a study schedule means developing a routine to learn various subjects.

MANTRA #142

Combine various sources: If you are learning a subject, never rely on one book; look into other resource material.

MANTRA #143

Form your view: You might be reading the notes from your teachers and peers; however, to excel, you need to have your perceptions.

MANTRA #144

Measure your progress: For effective learning, you must analyse your progress. When you measure your progress, you will know what you have learned until now and what needs to be learned more.

MANTRA #145

Develop emotional intelligence: Emotional intelligence means your ability to stay motivated and cope with stressful situations in any kind of learning environment.

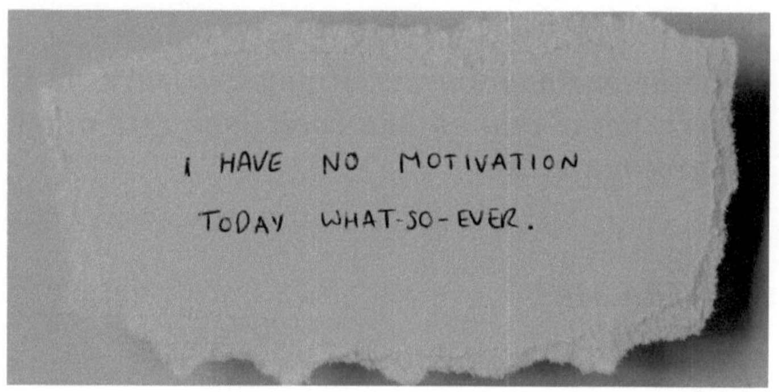

MANTRA #146

Avoid fixed mindset: You can never learn well with a predetermined attitude. If you belong to a fixed mindset, you will fixate on problems and feel overwhelmed.

MANTRA #147

Growth mindset. If you have a growth mindset, you will embrace challenges and treat them as a chance to learn new things.

MANTRA #148

EQ and IQ: To become a better learner, you need to have an emotional quotient (EQ) and intelligence quotient (IQ).

MANTRA #149

Don't compare yourself with others: When you compare yourself with people who know better than you, you will be discouraged from learning. Instead of comparison, focus on enhancing your knowledge of the subject you know better.

MANTRA #150

No shortcuts: You can impress your instructor by copying from your friends, the internet or elders. However, these kinds of acts will never make you knowledgeable.

ÞÞÞ

MANTRA #151

Enrol in "how to learn" courses: You might learn from traditional learning methods like reading, writing etc. However, for better learning effective learning, you need to be equipped with modern learning methods.

MANTRA #152

Learning is never-ending: You completed a course, but this is not an end to learning. You should continue to learn.

MANTRA #153

Be receptive to learning new things: Life is full of challenges. To overcome these challenges, you must always be willing to learn new things.

MANTRA #154

Teach to learn: It might sound weird. However, it is true. According to a study by Washington University, if you teach, you will know the subject better.

MANTRA #155

Don't just pass the test: The primary aim for many students is to get high scores and good grades. However, if you concentrate on just passing the exams, you will never have a better grasp of the subject matter.

MANTRA #156

Learning sessions: According to the experts at the Louisiana State University's Center for Academic Success, a learning session that is less than 30 minutes is not enough to learn the subject; likewise, if the session is longer than 50 minutes, the learners lose their interest.

MANTRA #157

Taking a short break between the learning sessions: Research has shown that if you study something for a specific time, take a break, and come back to look again, your brain will retain what you have learned.

MANTRA #158

Using mental spacing for effective learning: To learn better, you must study every day instead of reading throughout the day and never returning to the lesson. Repeating the task over and over for days will help you understand.

MANTRA #159

Take a study nap: According to a search published in Psychological science, downtime is essential when retaining what you have learned. Taking a short rest between the study sessions boosts your mental capacity.

MANTRA #160

Change your learning method: Using the learning method repeatedly might increase learners' boredom, whereas changing the plans will make learning exciting.

ᵖᵖᵖ

MANTRA #161

Interact with the subject and topics: The key to learning is how you interact with the issue and matters. You need multiple sources of information, and you need to interact with the data.

MANTRA #162

Ditch your learning style: If it is not working for you, ditch your learning method and embrace a new one. Don't stick to books only; gather videos, podcasts, movies, and blogs on the subject matter.

MANTRA #163

Make learning meaningful: You learned many things in your schools and colleges; how many of you remember those lessons? You remember only those lessons that matter in your life.

MANTRA #164

Learn by doing: Reading and listening are great ways to learn. However, you should never limit yourself to reading and listening; you also try to learn by doing it. You will never learn photography until you begin to take photographs.

MANTRA #165

Study the masters: Learning concepts and theories are essential. However, learning who propounded the ideas and vision is also fundamental. You will learn better if you find out how these concepts were developed.

MANTRA #166

Study the masters, practice what they have told you: You need to learn how the masters' did it; however, just knowing how they did it will not help you; you need to practice.

MANTRA #167

Learning through association: If you can associate the knowledge with something, you will understand it correctly.

MANTRA #168

Deliberate practice: Practice is a great way to learn. However, if you are more into the things you already know better, you are doing it wrong. You need to devote yourself to something you don't know or do not know much about.

MANTRA #169

Push yourself out of your comfort zone: To excel, you must push yourself out of your comfort zone. You should give more focus on things that you find difficult.

MANTRA #170

Find a mentor: It is easier to get to the next level quickly if you have a mentor. A mentor will offer you valuable perspective and experience that will improve your skills and knowledge.

ÞÞÞ

MANTRA #171

Be curious: Curiosity stimulates learning. You are interested means you are eager to learn.

MANTRA #172

Avoid procrastination: If you procrastinate, you are not learning anything new or learning at a slow speed.

MANTRA #173

Avoid laziness: Lazy individuals are not receptive to new knowledge and information. Inactivity will make you dull.

MANTRA #174

Focus on WH questions: The questions like why, who, when, where, and how will help you explore the concept for a better understanding.

MANTRA #175

Summarise what you have learned: If you can summarise what you have learned, it indicates that you have understood the subject matter well.

MANTRA #176

Highlight and make notes: As you read books on the subject matter, highlight the key points. A while later, you can go back to highlighted sections and directives. This will improve your understanding.

MANTRA #177

RightSuitable study materials: Having the right suitable study materials also aids learning. The proper study materials will make your learning process efficient. The books you choose should be the best book on the subject. Books are never enough; you also need notes and handouts.

MANTRA #178

Assessment through tests: If you participate in trials, you can learn how much you have learned. Tests will also show your strength and weakness.

MANTRA #179

School/college camps: Go to summer or winter camp. When learning is taken away from the classroom, it becomes fun. When a study does not look like studying and is more of an entertainment, the learner's ability to understand dramatically increases.

MANTRA #180

Afterschool programs: Afterschool programs offer creative learning methods. These programs are not just a way to entertain a child but also a creative way to introduce lessons.

ᢵᢵᢵ

MANTRA #181

Outdoor classrooms: These days, educators are taking education outside the school and giving more emphasis on outdoor classrooms. Learning becomes effective when it is blended with real life.

MANTRA #182

Learning from the community: Your emotional intelligence will improve if you are involved with community work. To be receptive to learning, you need high emotional intelligence.

MANTRA #183

Learn by play: Maria Montessori was an Italian educator who discovered how children learn better if they learn through games. This also applies to adults.

MANTRA #184

Learning space for better learning: To better understand the lesson or be eager to learn, the classroom environment should also be friendly. Students learn better if the classroom is well decorated.

MANTRA #185

Create valuable and relevant learning experiences: Individuals appreciate immediate relevancy. Therefore, learning will be effective if the learner can relate it to their lives and understand how they can use the knowledge.

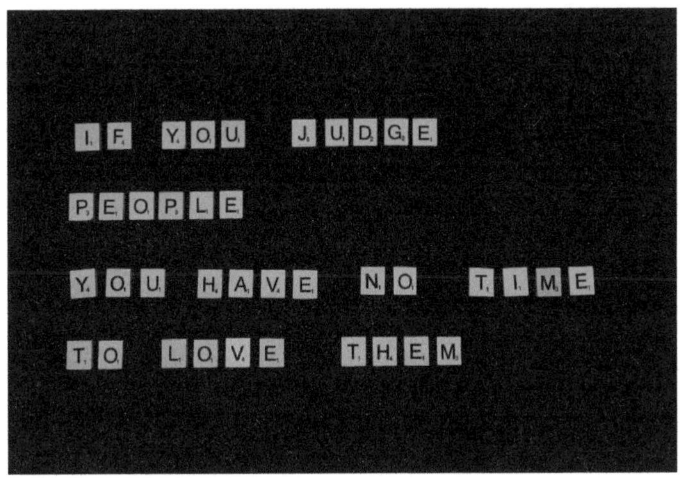

MANTRA #186

Focus on practicality: Generally speaking, people are not interested in learning theories; all they want to learn is how to enhance their knowledge and performance to excel in life.

MANTRA #187

Learning in mother tongue: Research has shown that if learner is allowed to learn in their mother tongue, they will perform better. Language should never become a barrier to learning.

MANTRA #188

A sense of humour for better learning: You don't have to make a serious face to learn. Likewise, the instructor should also have a good sense of humour to encourage learner participation in learning activities.

MANTRA #189

Suspense element for effective learning: Mystery invokes curiosity, and curiosity motivates the learner. If the instructor can introduce mystery (not giving everything in the first class), the learners will want to know more.

MANTRA #190

Individualised learning: All the learners do not have the same mental capacity. The learners will have a different understanding of the same lesson. Therefore, lessons should be individualised according to the learner's ability for better performance.

ꝒꝒꝒ

MANTRA #191

Know the benefit of learning: If the learner knows what he will benefit from learning this thing, he will be eager to learn.

MANTRA #192

Get the experience, not just the course: learning is not all about knowing the concept. Education is about knowing how to benefit from what you have learned. The learner should get the experience, not just the course.

MANTRA #193

Provide feedback immediately: If the instructor gives feedback directly, it will positively affect the learner. Feedbacks are a great way to inspire and stimulate the learner.

MANTRA #194

Constructive criticism: The learner needs criticism. However, criticism should come out as constructive criticism. The learner should be made aware of his strength and weakness.

MANTRA #195

Create an informal learning strategy: Learning does not have to be too formal. Learning becomes more effective in a relaxed learning environment.

MANTRA #196

Social learning: Learning becomes more effective when it is a collaborative exercise. Social learning will help you create a better learning experience.

MANTRA #197

Case studies: There is so much to learn from case studies. People like Darwin and Freud developed their theories from case studies.

MANTRA #198

Create sticky notes: make notes of essential points and post them on the wall or notice board. These notes will help you memorise the key issues.

MANTRA #199

Options are necessary to excel in the learning process: The learners should have an opportunity to choose what they want to learn. They will perform better if they can choose what they want to study.

MANTRA #200

Observation: Observation is a simple yet great way to learn. To learn something, you have to observe it systematically.

ᐅᐅᐅ

About The Authors

Dheeraj Mehrotra, MS, MPhil, PhD (Education Management) honoris causa., a white and a yellow belt in SIX SIGMA, a Certified NLP Business Diploma holder, is an

Educational Innovator, Author, with expertise in Six Sigma In Education, Academic Audits, Neuro-Linguistic Programming (NLP), Total Quality Management In Education, an Experiential Educator, a CBSE Resource towards School Assessment (SQAA), CCE, JIT, Five S, and KAIZEN. He has authored over 100 books on topics which include Computer Science, AI, Digital Body Language, NLP, Quality Circles, School Management, Classroom Effectiveness and Safety and security in schools. A former Principal at De Indian Public School, New Delhi, (INDIA), NPS International School, Guwahati, and Education Officer at GEMS, Gurgaon, with an ample teaching experience of over Two Decades, he is a certified Trainer for Quality Circles/ TQM in Education and QCI Standards for School Accreditation/ School Audits and Management.He has also been honoured with the President of India's National Teacher Award in the year 2006 and the Best Science Teacher State Award (By the Ministry of Science and Technology, State of UP), Innovation in Education for his inception of Six Sigma In Education by Education Watch, New Delhi and Education World- Best Teacher Award, BOLT Learner Teacher Award by Air India, 'Innovation in Education Award 2016' by Higher Education Forum (HEF), Gujarat Chapter, among others. He has developed over 150 FREE EDUCATIONAL MOBILE Apps for the Google Play Store exclusively for Teachers, Students, and Parents. This work has been recognised by the LIMCA BOOK OF RECORDS & INDIA BOOK OF RECORDS as the only Indian to draw that feast. Dr Mehrotra works as a PRINCIPAL at KUNWARS GLOBAL SCHOOL, Lucknow, in India. He has conducted over 1000 workshops globally on "Excellence In Education" integrated with Total Quality Management and Six Sigma,

Technology Integration in Education (TIE), Developing towards being ROCKSTAR TEACHERS, including Cyberspace, Cyber Security, Classroom Management, School Leadership & Management, and Innovative teaching within classrooms via Mind Maps, NLP and Experiential Learning in Academics. He is an active TEDx speaker and can be viewed on the youtube TEDx channel.As a premium UDEMY Instructor, he has developed over 450 courses and caters to over 8 Lakh students from 180 countries.He can be visited at www.authordheerajmehrotra.com.

***Madhukar Narrain has been an** Educator in Secondary School in Mauritius since 1978; he is also the Chairman of the Mauritian Society for Quality Control Circles - MSQCC and has been serving as a Director General of the World Council for Total Quality and Excellence in Education since 1999. He received the Gold Award of the Duke of Edinburgh International Award in 1978.*

He is the President of Mare DAlbert Arya Samaj & Member Arya Zila Samiti, Mauritius.

His former assignments include:

- *Chairman, Early Childhood Care and Education Authority (ECCEA) 2012 -2014*
- *Chairman, Mauritius Film Development Corporation 2003 -2005(MFDC)*
- *Director, Mauritius Duty-Free Paradise 2003 -2005*
- *Member of Environment Tribunal Appeal Board 1996 -1998*
- *Chairman of Mare D'Albert Village Council and Member of Grand Port Savanne District Council*
- *Community Health Leader, Mare DALbert Community Health Centre (Founder).*

ABOUT THE AUTHORS

"Be a student as long as you still have

something to learn, and this will mean all your life." — Henry L. Doherty

Printed by Libri Plureos GmbH in Hamburg,
Germany